Gallery Books

Editor Peter Fallon

DOUBLE NEGATIVE

Vona Groarke

DOUBLE NEGATIVE

Gallery Books

Double Negative
is first published
simultaneously in paperback
and in a clothbound edition
on 27 June 2019.

The Gallery Press
Loughcrew
Oldcastle
County Meath
Ireland

www.gallerypress.com

ISBN 978 1 91133 760 7 *paperback*
      978 1 91133 761 4 *clothbound*

A CIP catalogue record for this book
is available from the British Library.

Double Negative receives financial assistance
from the Arts Council.

Contents

To fill a Gap
Insert the Thing that caused it —
Block it up
With Other — and 'twill yawn the more —
You cannot solder an Abyss
With air —

Emily Dickinson, Poem No. 647

No one uses doilies anymore

so why do I hold the word to the window
so the holes in the pattern are years ago
and a visitor has come?

Impossible to talk of the mart or catarrh
as though days, clumps and clods of them,
could be glamoured by a paper doily
placed nicely on a plate.

Here, so, for this poem only,
is its wheel of stars
and star-shaped flowers,

an inkling of words
as ornament,
the way stars and, yes,
flowers are.

How Do We Get These Lives?

Being the question you'd strip to, if you could,
if the words came clear over a night
thinking itself a furnace
to be stoked repeatedly.

How riverly set it is on an answer
while pretending not to be. You reckon
you shouldn't have to reach for an ending
when they mostly seem to come so easily.

You want to be gentle, of course you do,
to slip through as your body does
the empty space before it and after
as you shift from day to day

but someone has stitched these little traps
like tiny mirror sequins to your clothes
so every time you move you think
you can't afford the glare.

When you shut your eyes it's as if
the white sheet all this flickers on
slips down an inch inside its clips
and the clips don't move at all.

Against Anxiety

A cartoon rider on a horse so real
it shits and stalls and rears against the rider
it's been saddled with in this narrative.

Who wonders, of course, if he's been here before
but nobody, not the old-timer in the sun chair
nor the woman stock-still in her parked car,
not even the dog that stares him down,
bids him the time of day.

The horse comes not to care.
There will be hay or else there won't;
either way, he's a horse still tomorrow.

The rider knows nothing about tomorrow.
He moves on, colour and storyline,
to the next bit of road and the next,
past fury, exhaustion and bafflement
as he drags with his ears a shaft of light
from a moon he thinks is real.

I suppose that's the thing about cartoons:
everyone sees the punchline coming
except the one who's about to get punched.

The way memory operates

is the way a man scheduled for hospital at two
at ten plants a rosebush by the wall
and asks not to be photographed
as he tamps the earth with the sole of his boot,
the inconceivable earth.

Small comfort that the rosebush dies,
that instead of roses all summer long
is the absence of roses year on year
shifting a little when the light is cramped
or rain huddles in from the west.

This too is the way I come back
to where I was young and my children were young,
to where we planted all those summers
and tamped the months around them, hard

and hard to say where the years have gone
when we lay down, night on night,

when the slipway sings so narrowly
and the wind stoppers up the gap in the wall
and the sky is civil in fits and starts
and the boats play their moorings like spoons.

Against Despair

When the past sets you down
between grillework and mirrors
closing off that one time

you feel for the hidden spring
but there's only a hinge
that whinges whenever you breathe.

Which is how the past remembers itself:
a faulty hinge and a lock that keeps turning
in a door that isn't there.

You believe it will turn into
something in the end
but it is you who changes

to a wooden boat out on a fathomless sea.
Which is how memory works,
what can you do?

The best you can hope for
is a warm day,
good news of this or that.

A Week in the Life of Dick and Jane, Who Met on the Internet

Sunday
On which we meet them powering down
their overly heartfelt screens.

Monday
He wonders if reserve or abandon would be less of a cliché.
She tells him no man has touched her this year.
Except for Mahler, of course.

Tuesday
His hand. Her hand. Their hands.
They are trying on Togetherness
the way they would a cloche or bowler
in a charity shop.

Wednesday
He imagines skylights.
She remembers rain.
See how they plan to make it work,
their glittery, foolproof plan?

Thursday
They play tennis. No, they don't.
They agree, as if lying on a bed of leaves,
that metaphor will be no use to them
when it comes down to it.

Friday
They decide to eat only yellow food.
On their fourth banana (each)
they admit they lack imagination,
acknowledge the need for their bodies
to hoik some other compromise.

Saturday
What shall we do with Dick and Jane:
shall we cluster, just so, in a happy ending?
Or shall we back out, line by line,
like a butler, having delivered the telegram
to a breathless drawing room?

This Poem

This is the poem that won't open
no matter where you press.

This is the poem that cries on street corners
and plays at being lost.

This is the poem arranged at a tilt
so all the words slide off.

This is the poem with lacquered roses
closing in on themselves after dark.

This is the poem that plays itself out
in dives in the small hours.

This poem likes to fool around
in other people's cars.

This poem gives away small coins
and winks at strangers' kids.

This is the poem that understands
what it is to be a dog.

This is the poem with a teensy tattoo
you'll never get to see.

This poem has no big plans for you,
which is something, as poems go.

Against Boredom

I marshal the kind of questions
answered by car parks, part songs and stained glass.
How you get from one to the next
is like chainmail
or sunlight on chainmail,
irrefutable.

Like that time when, for something to do,
I unhooked a screed of cloud,
laid it out over my bed,
let my hands imagine sea creatures
and new continents, a philosopher with a beard.

Whimsy? Perhaps. Or metaphor.
You choose.
I'm afraid I can't help you with that.

I am busy observing an evening scramble
over tall buildings, even mine,
through car parks and parked cars,
one blue eye fixed on loose talk,
one brown eye on the dark.

See how close I get?
And all without scarcely moving
except for my hands replacing,
minutely, a screed of cloud
on a backdrop of blue
that is anything but,

we all know that

though what else
could it be?

The Mancunian Way

Every seven seconds
the screen flips over a new ad

so the traffic blinks
and me, sat at my desk,

well, I blink too,

enough to wish seven seconds were eight
and eight a whole hour

so I could put my glasses on,
see the day come off its stilts,

shuffle into that parked, grey van
        and head on home.

Against Monotony

Today, a two-hundred mile drive and nothing
at the end of it but a glass of Merlot
and a radio fugue for voice and clarinet
which is a lot, when you think about it.

Oh, the squirrelling away of a snick of day
to come upon, unwontedly,
when the drive is polished concrete
and the playing fields, pure quartz:

that, right there, is a trick worth playing,
the kind of dark-blue, offhand trick
to be played maybe the once, and gently,
so you get away with it.

As If Anything Could

A paper from the year before last is the start
of my tonight fire. Where was I? What have I done?
It's not as if the world was shouting, 'Do this!' or
'Do this!' at me. And it's not as if learning one thing
means unlearning one thing else. Home is to lie
when you need to lie, a bowl of tomorrow left
by the bed and a window at the height of your hand
to open, like a diary, so the days and all their equipage
slip lightly, oh so lightly, from the room.

On the Deployment of Simile to Understand Good Marriages

Clothes stiffening into position overnight
on chairs or on the backs of chairs —
that is like a marriage too

and so is the rain crowding the window
so hard I can hardly see through

and so is the sand in the rockpool
when the stick in your hand
or the stone thrown by you
is a thing of the past

so the sand settles back
as before

what is obvious

is how the rock hides
inside itself

right there
in front of you.

The Making of Porcelain

It will need to be a thousand years old
and warmed by the rising sun, this clay,
chilled by only full moons. I will need
river water never broken over a wet stone
and hands that fit inside my skin,
my eyes to be glazed with robin's egg glaze
and the blood in my veins to be ox-blood
for the hour of my doing.

The bowl I make I will hold in my mouth
until a name for it balances on the lip
and then I will place it in the nape of my life
so it knows more than I do.

This will be what I make of my time,
a bowl I gift to you. Look underneath,
where the war came close is a smidge
the shape of the scar on my knee
which is also the curve of the bend in the road
that leads to the rim of the sea.

You could fill this bowl to the brim with ice
or sunlight, and put every promise you made
in there, and squares of paper on which you have written
lines from love poems and names of stars
and boardwalks and childhoods and mothers in coats.
You could put in driftwood and your lapis ring,
last night's dreams and tonight's, undreamt,

it doesn't matter, for whatever you place inside this bowl
will not be there when you look again.
This is the beauty of the finishing touch
applied with a brush made from your lost years:

come morning, each morning,
when you rise to the light
and think to see what remains to be seen,
the moonlight glaze I chose for you
has undone everything.

Against Loneliness

Time was, the rain brought nasturtiums, like a lover,
but now is not August anymore
and the rain comes empty-handed
which is fine by me.

There are so many flowers already,
so many spoons and shoes and candlesticks
to be accounted for.

I make lists for company
of all the objects in the world
that bloom the way nasturtiums do,
loudly, brazenly.

The rain doesn't care so much for lists.
Tonight it calls by the house late
with something important to say.

Its words end in all double letters
that lean in, like italics,
close to each other
so nothing comes between.

Vanishing Point

Sometimes the van was the colour of the field.
I was small then, barely eleven, and every day
that summer was taller, more sure of itself than I.
The silver grass of the lawn, uncut, used to wait
for the moon to pass, sitting out by the wall
to tilt up its face as if laughing, to shake out its long hair.
No one could say I lacked imagination: the ferns
were all the time wagging spindly, elderly fingers at me.

Once a man caught my eye in the village:
his were not the colour of the van or the field.
He said nothing to me and I hoarded it, that nothing,
hoard it still, nights the wind blows from the east
with its city talk a-glitter like fine rain in headlights.

Sometimes I want to tell it this way but the want
to tell it just this way is only as strong
as the want to tell it every other way.

Against Darkness

In the museum of the photographer's studio
I find I cannot breathe.
The room is light-tight, clogged
and hellish, this stepping around the props
and costumes and lamps and cameras.
There are too many of us.

The photo of the little boy
has a toy horse in it and, yes,
here is that horse six decades on
only this time I am the little boy
perched and primed for the record now
and we all know what happened to him.

What I Didn't Know Then About the World

I had a yellow dress that summer
but the mountain, in its so many greens,
put it about that I was not what I seemed,
said in its feathery, wind-flipped way:
only one of us needs to be naked here
and I don't see why it should be me.

Against Pessimism

I remember there was a big bridge
with a toll and I didn't have change.
The river was a shadow of itself below
and a thin white cloud kept time with us
to the other side.

I fell asleep. Later someone, probably Sophie,
said, 'she fell asleep'
and that's as much as it amounts to
when you think about it.

Sophie took me to a fortune teller
who said my grandma would die in a fire
and would leave me everything.

Both my grandmas had already died
their bone-cold deaths, long before.
So much for fortunes. So much for fire.
I don't know where Sophie is now.

Back then the future was the bridge
but somewhere it changed to the toll.
You hand over coins, he hands back smaller coins.
He doesn't speak so you don't either,
just look ahead, release the brake,
get underway.

How the Past Depends on Detail for Effect

The whole night the same two sounds
lob back and forth, traffic and waves,
and now and then, from underneath,
a voice last wound up decades past
surfaces as in a dream
and all the seashells in the jar
have faces with mouths shaped Now or Then
and my mother wears her turquoise dress
with yellow flowers at the neck
falling from the hem
to be gathered by my father
in a light blue bag
that has in it that I can see
the road with all its cars and noise
and, furthermore, the sea.

Stone Trees

This is not a small poem about loss or disappointment.
This is a runnel with no use for a bridge, a curtain wall
with no dead load, a road with no bend to my door. This
is a forest with no trees. This cannot be foreseen.

This is me, opening my mother's spool box, taking time
to task. Here is her thread, her wherewithal,
filoselle from reeled silk, crewel yarn, cotton floss.
Here is her hand before decades of death, holding a needle

against the white page, flicking noun to verb, as she did me.
And this is me rounding on middle age, still thinking,
what should I do? Hours stack up like saucers on a shelf
and my to-do list unravels like a tin song off the radio.

I am listening to a night fix me between pert notes of a bird
I keep meaning to look up and the jollity of wind chimes
I would like to snap in my hands. Instead, grant me, if you will,
the certainty of some hard facts to make sense of what I do here.

One: there are days that lie and days that tell the truth.
Two: pain has its own music that is neither starry nor trite.
Three: in Arizona, in the painted desert, live trees agatized
to amethyst, jasper, and chalcedony. I read this and find

(of course) a metaphor for thickening blood and marrow,
for the fact of age. It takes centuries, more than lives,
and who knows the difference between loss and accrual
over so much time? All life in those trees culminates

in the glittery consonants of topaz and quartz
as if only words with hard endings could hold sway.
I'm not sure what will happen next, though it may yet
prove to be something as ruthless as it is absolute.

It would be easy to give up, to let the facts of our lives
stiffen to an obvious kind of truth. But we do not.
My mother never sewed — the spool box was for optimism,
it had no winter in it. Even stone trees come to their own

breathtaking conclusion. Death, for all its pretty names
and intricate patterns, holds us to a promise we made
never to flinch from what time does to the quick of us,
turning ourselves, our very selves, into astonishment.

Poem with My Mother and Frank O'Hara

Today I am channelling Frank O'Hara
(my mother's second cousin
once removed).
I pick up a detail and I put it down
and I call that poetry.

I'm so pleased with myself
I forgive the orchid for dying,
the orchid I bought to replace the dog
that had replaced a dog with the same name
from my childhood, who can't have been
replacing anything that I know about.

I'm so pleased with myself
I almost forget today is a sick day
and the old woman with the knotty fingers
has been crocheting my lungs in neon green.

It's the only colour she uses
and only on days when the sign for the Emerald Bar
flips on, though she's not been to the Emerald Bar.
I imagine it, counter and tables and stools
covered in lichen and reeking of funerals
as she does, when she visits,
to sit on the sofa and never speak and crochet morosely.

She's the kind of woman who eats eight grains of rice
in a bowl of steam for lunch.
I don't like her. And I don't like
how the skin she makes me wear all day
is a size too small and the colour reminds me
of the toilet floor in the Emerald Bar after closing time.

She makes me feel like 'ratchet' sounds.

When I work this out
I'm so very pleased with myself
I take a penknife to her wool,
cut it to hyphens and sprinkle them,
like maggots, on this page.

Then I stop coughing
and hearing my heartbeat whooshing
in my right ear,
stop thinking I'm me
before I was born
and I am in my mother now
and that's the end of that.

Against Loss

With the dribs and drabs
of saxophone music
from way over the lake

comes you in your young day
(one glimpse only),

'20s bob and '20s bones
(dear bones
knitted by hands from home),

comes you, posed
between light on water
and these same trees in light.

Oh, little girl with the sun in your eyes,
where did you go?
Where did everyone go?

As ever, Sunday morning

is a stained glass window
all high notes and accord
to be acknowledged inside eyelids,
felt where feeling is, on the tip of the tongue,
in the small of the small of day.

It's a notion. But there are only
these few elastic hours
for the week to recover
to absolve itself, re-boot.
That I am not as young as the morning

is known even to the weather
which knows everything.
The sky flops down on skylights
as if they were old chairs
with crochet cushion covers

and I play my joints like a castanet
with a hairline crack.
My body, grief colander, shows me how
to think of time as what keeps
the machine of me functioning

so I find I am grateful for colour still,
for the single bright blue earring,
the yellow cloud, the white sheet
that covers me all, including my silence
(its petty blood-swarm),

the mirror's one-liners
and both these hours pinned to half a bed,
how they fulfil their own outline
pulling a barely visible thread
out of the quick of what isn't there.

Against Harm

for Tommy, in Moscow

The mind tightens once, at 3 a.m., like a butterfly screw
and I am nubbed in the lull
as a world heron-still in its put-on innocence.

My home, as if braced for high winds —
windows cowering in their window frames,
the roof pulling night around it
like a knotwork shawl —
would have me backed into fear
it caulks between these pointed hours.

The room you don't sleep in alongside my own
is eons of recall and small hours and rain,
into the corners of which I cram
like newspaper into damp walking boots
every night-spawned fret, news barb and threat
that slumps into or is feathered by
the safe I cannot keep you.

Bloodless trees, rook-choked, are notes
on a stave of wires up the street
I can't even see. That your breath
should refute those notes but can't
is another rain-spattered fact I count
as I count the miles between us
rounded up to the nearest thousand,
to the full of your not being here.

Instead, so, of a streetlamp flooding
the empty skylight above your bed,
here, love, if you have light to read by,
is a paper moon for you from home,
its length and breadth a long, lit path:

every thousand miles, one footstep,
every thousand hours, one breath.

On Seeing Charlotte Brontë's Underwear with My Daughter in Haworth

With bad weather forecast and light silting up in cramped windows we are the only visitors. The year settles in a corner of the room, has removed its white gloves, tip by tip, and set to one side its summer purse of bibelots and sheen.

Half-term of her final year, we are sightseers intent on moors. In the morning her windcheater and red wellies will bestow the dust of summer festivals upon sullen, wind-soaked sheep.

We will park and walk ourselves into the final, cutting rain between pages of her favourite book. She wants to go all the way to Top Withens, or the house they say must have been Top Withens, given its loneliness and set.

But now is artefacts and souvenirs: a perfume with too much musk in it, a jar of damson jam which we probably won't open until past its sell-by date.

We are buying the word 'damson'. And we are buying time.

'Are they real?' she asks me, and I watch her reckon the distance between what should and should never be seen. We have fallen short.

She draws, and what she draws is rain falling slant inside the bedroom; the bed as a box of leaves and stones and, within the display case, she hangs from the clothes rail little moons.

On the mannequin water lilies stand in for morning dress, and the backdrop is marbled in what looks to me like veins and arteries. But when I flick through the sketchpad in the B&B all the pages, what is left of them, are clean.

Next day she leaves it in the car. When she moves away she will leave it again, a sketchpad with no name on it and only the faintest traces of where she made skies of darned linen, and unfastened every stitch.

Against Nostalgia

Beryl, Shirley, Doris, Gail,
names that fell like coins between floorboards
or pins for hairdos past the height of fashion even then,

all lost, all unaccounted for,
except on this wayward Sunday hour,
their bosoms shoring up the gallery wall.

Oh, you women with your private shillings
and songs smuggled out of your young day
into mint-green kitchens with lino floors,

a soda loaf cooling on a wire rack,
the fire set first thing for evening
and a place for everything.

Oh, you women with your bunions and bills,
your horn-rimmed spectacles and missing back teeth,
your handbags and small change and single key.

Oh, you women in your fur-collared coats,
counting on them to remember your bodies
as your bodies remember your lives.

Oh, what did you think the days were for
that lodged, like pips, in the flesh of your throats
as if you were, somehow, fruit?

Vintage

Between trains I kill an hour
with '70s ceramic coffee pots
and Scott Walker LPs
while Doris Day, in clip-on earrings,
is innocent on a loop.
I try on buttoned evening gloves
and plunge my hand in mink.
When did I start sleeping with the light on?

Out on the headland, from the train, a boat full of rain.

The Lash

When you finally tease it from your inner eye
the lash is grey (which is maybe why you spent
last evening lid-fidgetting a guerrilla itch)
and looks like nothing on your fingertip
except this little fucker is the future now
and it knows all about you.

Against Age

Feeling my way to the brim of a room

I find how the sapling lines up
with the light cord

how the sky has so much linen in it

or the white wall two-steps
the bedframe

almost solve

how the cramps in my body
answer to nothing,

a fist of blood pulling
gently, roughly

all the way back from me.

For Real

For the summer of forty-six days on the trot of never a drop of rain; the summer of subsidence, of wheels snared and joggers snagged and even a bed with a man in it who wakes to the bottom of a sinkhole and thinks he has died, but has not.

For the summer of hot air and noise; news like vuvuzelas blaring over tangled air.

For the earth so needled by drought it gives up a henge not seen for centuries, postholes and causeway clear as day, if day is the forty-sixth without rain. And here it is, conjured by light dry as bone and a summer thousands years old.

For the last of the Brazilian tribe filmed hunting in his forest. For the hole he stretches his hammock over that rhymes with five other dark holes. For the hammock pulled between the tree he must have a name for and the point of these spare words.

For the skittish fire out on the moors stopping at nothing until, like a debutante, it exhausts itself with showing off; forgettable, nearly, once the photos look samey, but for smut on baths under skylights, or windscreens' skim of char.

For further fires, more vicious, with whole towns in their maw. But I can't think about that: I would only start imagining what I've no right to.

For the luxury of scruples about appropriate empathy.

For the open mouths of awful fish and the rhyme, slant rhyme, with the halo of the alley lamp and the bullet hole in the thigh of a child caught stealing two from the man who guards his fish with a gun, who would lock the ocean if he could be sure he owned the key.

For all this talk of borders; for the wee man whose job it is to spray it on roads and ditches, through whins and rivers, over meadows and braes; and then the next week, when the wind shifts, to come out at dawn from a hole in the ground and spray those whimsical red lines blue or green again.

For the city of gravel where there used to be the city of tents and gardens sewn in cans and bottles under cardboard signs with the names of the missing, the lost.

For the blood moon, how it slots into metaphor like a sideshow trick involving sleight of hand, dry ice, a torch and blood-red filter.

For the earth, never full, for all we cram in versions of ourselves (but not ourselves, who level out the soil above them with unmended boots).

For the evening, for once and only, easy in itself, draped across the chaise of the Bay, buttons loosened and hair unpinned, all its blues losing the run of themselves amid talk of the door of tomorrow being open wide, first thing.

For the other Bay, leagues behind this one, where there is no repose and certainly no Edwardian metaphor, where searchlights pick up lifejackets or a hand in motion, or mouths fill with saltwater what should be a scream.

For the hill that seems to be ashamed, the way it stands with its back to the world or cowers against reprimands it expects always, like rain.

For the saplings that crowd where the earth was scorched, not knowing how useless they are. You could call it comfort, the way a wife would touch her husband's cheek; or a husband would his wife's.

For the room that gives on the darkening hill, my body in it like a coin in a drawer opened by a secret spring.

For the waiting. For the years that burn like wood dried carefully.

For the interval between cars on the road, as long as I hold my breath.

For the night you're the only car on the road, light still in the west after dark. And nobody knows where you are, you are. Nobody knows where you are.

For your passport and your mobile phone, your idea of safety.

For settling on kindness for a finish, on a way to tell it true.

For the girl who loves today more than yesterday, because today is the light blue dress.

For you, because we have come this far. For the distance. For the road.

For the blue dress, yours for the asking.

For all the good it will do.

Against Vanity

Coming, a field flooded in the middle
gave the glad eye to the world.

Here the carpark brims with darkness.
My room forgets about me.

No drier tinder than hours gathered
from the floor of hotel rooms.

Self-storage

When I send my past to the lock-up
in fifteen numbered, see-through boxes
that two men lug down five flights
and hoist into an unmarked van
I should feel released, sprung

from a twenty-five year sentence
played out backwards, sent down at the end
right before the bad thing happens
but after the time has been served.
And I nearly do. I do.

I commit myself to month after month,
paid in advance, and they hand me
two sets of keys to a padlock
they will secure once the better part
of me is safe inside.

In drizzle (as the past must be)
the man with the limp secures the back
while the bald one has me sign,
says he will text the unit number
so I know where I am.

The bedroom closes over where
the boxes used to be and the mirror
has me in it, or what's left of me,
sitting down to this clean slate
with my news and news and news.

Against Sorrow

Behind the rain knotting silver wool
into streamers out the back

and before an ocean laying down the law,
as ever, in the front

is me in an opera of silence
in a borrowed, light blue room;

all my intervals done with,
the curtains tightly drawn.

The Old Country

I came out of that country
with one suitcase
crammed with newspaper,
seeds in every fold.

No. That's not it.

No seeds and no newspaper.
My suitcase was full of snow
and the shadow of snow

which is another way of saying
it was full of lies.

I had been there for years,
whole months of them.

And then, just like that,
words stopped calling on me,
street signs flipped inside out.

My neighbours swopped faces.
The blue door was, by nightfall,
paler blue. On clean days hail
pockmarked the pillows.

I try not to picture it.

Or to calculate heartbeats,
blood I bled, rooms undressed,
ways of waking up, ounces
in an ounce of love.

I am scattering ink-white ashes as I write.

Sometimes you live a day
so it passes through you
like a ghost on the landing

and sometimes I think
there is no landing
and the ghost cannot be me.

Against Earnestness

The morning skiffles its every tint and blemish,
if blemish it is, so the set of my window is of a piece
with a skirmish of magpies on a tin, green roof
or trees in tatters over the path or a shrub I pin down
in scant words, that the day makes flitters of.

Nothing sticks, my eyes tire of this so much world.
The hours have little to show for themselves
but trinket themes and false starts,
a jade bracelet, if jade it is, hung in front
of an open window, to set the day to 'Go'.

The Picture Window

The ocean can't seem to stop itself
wishing in a thousandth of green ink
to find, behind the red hot pokers,
a sunspot where it might rest for an hour,
there to settle on its shoulders
the tatty turquoise shawl I brought,
embroidered with tin ships,

there to beg me to move my chair
to where it can keep an eye on me
and to stop for a minute in my whole life
that humming of infernal darkness
I practise in years of nights,
to just sit quietly, if I please,
and listen to the stones.

And so I do. The window opens on the bay.
The gate tells fairy stories about every wink of wind
which the cabbage tree thinks are nonsense,
just as everything is. And I,
with my tongue behind my teeth
and my feet in their fathoms of pile
and my razorbill fingers to comb the rain,

I wait as the keyhole waits
for the ocean to get up from its white chair,
shuck off these silky metaphors
and, cursing my every idleness,
take itself off down the shingle path
that, obsequizing every step,
has nothing, all the while, to say to me.

Against Apathy

For five days, a house on a cliff, on loan.
My job, to gather seaspray and sand into something
to hold up to my home, oh, half a world away.
I settle in, make friends with the fridge, the heater
and the view. We are never on our own-ey-o for long.

When the hot water won't work I make to go next door,
to Toby (as the note said I should) to ask for help.
But just when I'm walking over in my head,
giving my name and explanation, putting between us
the notion of my body in the shower (oh god),
it comes right, hot water fresh from the tap
like a small child being tickled all over
and all I want in the world is to say to Toby,
'Hot water from the tap, my friend — now, isn't that a thing?'

But, oh, you know. I let it be another quiet day.
My shower drains the boiler and I listen to it fill.
Also, I oil the house keys for company,
smell my clean arm every minute,
keep time by Toby's ins and outs

and an ocean and a ticking softwood stove
keep time with me.

The House With No Clocks

The days are long and leisured
but the years, the years
pass by like the dark swoop of the stingray
as it slides under the jetty.
— Sarah Broom, 'The Years'

Sea at the front, wind at the back,
the run of the house with the grapefruit tree
has been given to me. Mine for five days
this stack of wood, this patchwork quilt,
the keys with the dolphin key ring,
all this giddy rain.

Mine to sleep on a borrowed bed,
to measure my nights by the measure
of what another life has been
as though one could line up moon
and stars, tally them by fireglow,
breathe in light years between.

Mine to know what to do next,
how to make good on days that close
as darkness closes when a car
drives through. Mine the bare bones
of a quiet hour, then the skitter of words
tipped by the wind when a roof leans into it.

Mine to reckon an equals sign
with my own black pen.
Mine the space to either side,
mine the pivot, mine the promise,
mine the stumble, mine the sway,
mine, thousands of time.

The Blue Mountains, New South Wales

Winter, but you wouldn't think it,
the kind with jonquils and lily of the valley,
a frilly darkness fussing round the clean edge

of daylight. I have given myself June
and with it, a year with two shortest days,
not much of a summer to speak of.

Yesterday, at the Winter Magic Festival,
a samba band followed the Hari Krishnas
in a tie-dyed rumpus not a million miles

from what the cockatoos and lyrebirds
are up to in the gumtree. I walk past
into an afternoon with a wall in it

and run my finger over the top
to feel it hand up smooth, round hours,
stone after lacework stone.

It falls through me, the day, and no word
of mine can snag or stall it. What matter.
Under quilted hearts I dream myself back

to the bowl of morning
turned upside down,
light clattering out of it.

Take light, for instance,

shaking itself out of the valley
like a dog coming out of the sea

and me, jet-lagged and pinched
oh, way too early,
onto the raised deck up in the trees,

the kind of trees I knew
two cities and a life ago

watching, quiet as I can, until the birds come
within an inch of me
and the traffic soaks itself up, wet sponge,

and my pen, stalling, brands its shadow
on next door's garage roof.

Ninety-nine days on the trot, maybe,
that skinny tree flicks on its glitz
for a morning that couldn't care less

but this day, day one hundred,
is for me.

Against Disappointment

The pigeon that ousted the mistle thrush
on my winter balcony

who'd drop me runs of speckled song
in return for handfuls of crumbs:

this pigeon, for all my knocking and shooing,
thinks he owns the place.

He is waiting for me to leave out bread
and I am waiting for him to be a mistle thrush.

That's the way of it these days.
I could crack the code

if I knew what it meant,
but what would I do then?

What It Feels Like Is No Way The Same As How It Feels

Let's agree I'm crouched behind a hedge
with voices approaching, a woman and man.

They come closer so I make bodies of them,
his hand around her waist; her gold earrings.

They are yellow behind the green
so the day is lit by them laughing,

then it's not

and there's only the hedge for company,
a hedge all full of itself.

Against Melancholy

Such a storm to have me by the throat.
Well, it's not as if I went looking for it
or, honestly, put much store by its antics,
all those camera-ready tricks.

So I change the bedlinen for the turquoise set,
imagine I'm wearing a sky-blue dress
and the sun has come down off its high horse
and my friends are waiting for me.

There now. Seems I stared it down.
Let the evening shake itself dry like a dog
so the tail is the last thing wriggiggling
as, of course, you knew it would be.

A to Z

Say one thing and straight away the opposite
hoves into view. This is why, perhaps, I am
indefinite — something to do with being Libran
or being short and therefore always riddled with
comparative fact. Connections go over my head
or slip through my hands or I stow them away
at the back of my mind, where knowing what
to do with them next is a matter of perspective
and, yes, scale. We are so small. We put tins
in cupboards and we take them out again.
We forget to eat. We eat. We love.
We only wish we could.

But if there's a me and also a we,
then there must be a you. There you are,
one shoelace open, on a bench in a park
with a breathtaking view, as you imagine me
into your hand. And there I am, cupped
as a hailstone or a hailstone's worth of rain,
until this is a story, then an anecdote.
Then, not even that.

Against Caprice

It ought to sound discouraged, snow shift on the skylight,
so where did it get that silvery tone, those French vowels,
lit as the tip of a cigarette in a '40s film? How come
it knows to be ritzy when today is packed in grey?
The red blind lifted on the forecast, as it had to do.
First snow, then hail, then rain so the ribs of the hill
began to poke through. Strange to think of snow as flesh;
strange as ever, this shift of words, its skylit tilt and slip.

Odd company you find you keep: a stranger staring down fire
in your grate, no idea how he got here or how long he'll stick.
Seems he has a key, dibs on a chair, nothing to say for himself.
Not when the fire shifts, not when the snow. Not as the hill
is being lost to you both, him pulling down the red blind.

Writing My Way In

You, I knew from the rhyme of the white lamp
   and the full moon.
You, I knew from the card with the woodcut,
   here longer than ever you were.
You, I knew from the salt on the counter,
   the letters I'd make of it.

What I didn't know I learned.
Your voice was a wrought iron gate, I said,
with a narrow road behind it.

And the metaphor told me two separate things,
neither with a weight of darkness,
only one of them about you.

On *Reading* Love Poems of the Irish

Like a flat stone over lake water
love skims eleven centuries,
skittering over whole stretches of time
(including the fallows of your life and mine),
snagging the surface of, oh, now and then
so the deep is riddled with fine words and rings,
and no stone to speak of.

Against Untruth

The teaspoon knows a lie when it hears one.
If I could unspool its many circuits
of that innocent teacup
and lay them end to end and fastened

it could maybe be some kind of bind
to tighten round the quick of it
for as long as it takes to make it stop
and half as long again.

The Light Blue Door

Of course I wanted to live with you
in the house with the light blue door
perched on the headland like a seagull
eyeing the notion of flight
in a sky crammed with elsewhere.

As if we could. And yet here we are.
The wind with its pocketful of names
follows us room by room
and always a late-May kind of light
floods winter in our mouths.

You're not even here any longer
and I too am long gone.
So who's that in the armchair, head in hands,
and who's that running for clothes on the line,
night coming down on it all?

Against Rancour

A car ascending the back of the hill
pushes a cart of light

in which all manner of gee-gaws
such as aeroplanes and stars

rattle above the little noise
of keyholes and doors not fully closed

and curtains that can't bring themselves
to meet.

Which is where I put you
with your back to me

clocking how one panel of darkness
slides back to let the village pass

through the eye of night;
how it is rammed shut again

as the car tips over
the tipping point

down into Hill Street
as you turn back

to your lit room.
And all our lives go on.

The Choosing

Under the poem's branches two people
Walk and even the words are shy.
      — W S Graham, 'The Secret Name'

Well then, let morning be a pair of yellow boots
drilling into the edge of the wood.
Or have it be the wood with the yellow boots
lining everything up to their stride.
Either way we get where we're going
or else, lost, footless, doubling back,
we decide those two words on that tree stump
were left there for us two to find.

So take it from me this morning, do,
two second-hand, blue-veined possible roads —
one for the forest, one for the shore.
Between them, the choosing. And us.

Through the forest on one side is visible
a field lit by sunflowers or rape;
the other side has its back to the field
and shoulders a darkness with two sounds in it —
a yellowhammer and a woodpecker
that hammers out, insistently,
the news that everything will be wonderful
or else that everything won't.
That either the trees will shelter you
as you huddle with your dry words
or they'll crowd your head
so no light gets through

until your fingers separate the branches,
flip back the clumped hammers
on your Underwood
or lately hit RTN on Word

so the screen yawns wide
as a clearing my day
falls hard into, like rain.

Cup-marks

I drove down England, Lancs to Wilts,
through names lit as metal in sunlight,
along motorways and slip roads, the radio
flicking songs to ghosts under every
flyover.

That night the heat coming off the stones
was like something banked against the chance
of a capable hand once clearing out
a hairline crack or covert ruck to simply prise it
open.

I walked among them, feeling my way, the way
their hoard of years was a ritual patience,
how the clasp and hoist of standing stones
rendered them funerary, at a loss, this last
of August,

its winnowed and held breath
coming again as bits of torch songs
remembered by rain, so the cup-marks
sustain the air between their burden
and refrain.

It would fall to me only to attend, as when,
by moonlight or some other device,
the music of stones stills in my hand
before sweeping back into itself the slight
I am

that still requires to listen, because it's what
there's left to do, for the pure note of axes
being polished on stone, for the hefting
of greywether into sockets prepared rightfully
and true,

then the peeling back of guide ropes,
the whole shift and commotion of the move
capsizing into silence, to the purlieu of a passage
between two lines, one circle circling another,
in mind

before anyone thought to hew verbs from them,
to furrow the rhyme of sarsen and moss
and to make something of it, as cup-marks scooped
by river stones make something of
the river.

This Being Still

1

With the dog's head on my foot, asleep,
it seems wrong to move.

She is getting old, doddery,
walks into doors and stumbles off kerbs,
feels her way by the edge of my voice.

I have brought her to an island
of cropped light and few words,
her silence just as diffuse as my own.

She keeps close into me.

It is a small gift to the world,
I reckon, this our being still.

2

In no time, at the clatter of a winter bird
or my book falling or the heat kicking in,

she will rise to the surface
of the last of day

and I will meet her milky gaze
to wonder what I wanted

to begin with.

Aftermath Epigrams

I breathe in. Nothing happens.
That's good, isn't it?

~

Onion-papered first light,
a page of black behind it
for effect.

~

Under a skylight
pebbledashed with rain
the radio bleats its new day news.
This is the world
and this is the world.
Oh, the circles I move in.

~

From annal to analysis:
every day is words blindfolded
and made to walk the plank.

~

The clouds are determined
to put me in mind
of who I used to know.

~

My phone rings.
Two crows scoot

from one wire
to another.

~

Silence in a room before a telephone call
is very different
from the silence after.

~

The finch on my patio
brings news of the future.
I am of the world.

~

Some islands, migration happens overnight.
One August morning you wake and all
the kittiwakes and guillemots are gone.
From then it's a riot of silence
where the backdrop used to be.

~

I inhale the fumes of cars on the bridge.
Who says I live alone?

~

Aloneness isn't in it,
say the berries,
say the tea leaves,
says the moth.

~

The houseplants
are a tenacity
I take
as an affront.

~

Day to day
like a handrail
for teetering by.

~

The city is hoarse
from singing
all those lullabies
to me.

~

Silence, sullen and implacable,
growing as mould on a lemon,
as mould on a nectarine.

~

Not the ghost on the landing.
Not the ghost on the stairs,
but the ghost with his fist in my mouth.

~

If it's a poem
it should have people in it.
I don't see anyone.

~

But there's no point
whatsoever
in trying to punish the world.

~

If it's to be words for company
it would be really helpful, thanks,
if they had something civil to say.

~

Are you just going to lie there all morning
thinking yourself into red fuzz?
Who cares? My hand cares.
Who says? Not me.

~

A whole day transcribed for tuba
and played down a coalmine.

~

Yesterday's headache saps colour from today
so I am grateful for a yellow coat
resetting the street to winter
and its many opposites.

~

A child in a stroller smiles back at me.
I am visible.

~

A day without a volta
is a day with nowhere to hide.

~

Small words on a page not a whole lot
bigger than themselves.
Use a metal ruler.
Is this finally enough?

Acknowledgements

Acknowledgements are due to the editors of the following publications where some of these poems, or versions of them, were published first: *The Dark Horse, The Irish Times, The New York Review of Books, PN Review, Ploughshares, Poetry, Poetry Ireland Review, Poetry London, Poetry Salzburg, The Threepenny Review, The Well Review* and *Yale Review*. 'This Poem' was published in *The New Yorker*.

'The Choosing' was commissioned for *The Caught Habits of Language: An Entertainment for W S Graham for Him Having Reached One Hundred* (Donut Press, 2018, eds. Rachael Boast, Andy Ching and Nathan Hamilton).

'The Making of Porcelain' was commissioned for *Make Believe* (A Journal about Craft and Creativity).

The epigraph to 'The House With No Clocks' is taken from Sarah Broom's *Tigers at Awhitu* (Carcanet Press, 2010).

Thanks to the Heinrich Böll Cottage on Achill Island for a residency there in January 2015, and to Varuna, The Writers' House in New South Wales, Australia, for a residency in June 2015.

Special thanks are due to the University of Manchester and to the Cullman Center at the New York Public Library for their invaluable support in the completion of this book.

To John McAuliffe, Michelle O'Sullivan and Nick Laird, careful and generous readers, my warm thanks. And to The Gallery Press, as ever, for all they do.